Growing Up with SAME-SEX PARENTS

Zack's Story

Keith Elliot Greenberg
Photographs by Carol Halebian

LERNER PUBLICATIONS COMPANY / MINNEAPOLIS

The poem on page 15 by Aylette Jenness is used with permission of the author.

Illustrations by John Erste

LIBRARY OF CONGRESS CATALOGING-IN-PUBLICATION DATA

Greenberg, Keith Elliot.
    Zack's Story : growing up with same-sex parents / Keith Elliot Greenberg ; photographs by Carol Halebian.
      p. cm.
    Includes bibliographical references.
    Summary: An eleven-year-old boy describes life as part of a family made up of himself, his mother and her lesbian partner.
    ISBN 0-3225-2581-X (alk. paper)
    1. Children of gay parents—Juvenile literature. 2. Lesbian mothers—Juvenile literature. 3. Mothers and sons—Juvenile literature. 4. Homosexuality—Juvenile literature. [1. Mothers and sons. 2. Gay parents. 3. Lesbians. 4. Family. 5. Homosexuality.] I. Halebian, Carol, ill. II. Title.
HQ777.8.G74 1996
306.874—dc20   96-33855

Manufactured in the United States of America
1 2 3 4 5 6 – JR – 01 00 99 98 97 96

CONTENTS

LAST WEEK, MY FRIEND ALEX and I were sitting on the
steps talking, and we saw my mom and Margie coming
toward us. Margie lives with me and my mom. I call her my
second mother.

My mom couldn't hear what we were talking about, but I
could tell she was curious. When she and Margie reached
the steps, my friend and I quit talking. "What's going on?"
my mom asked.

Alex said, "I wanted to know if it's all right if I told someone that you're a lesbian."

My mom looked at Margie, and then they both laughed. "Sure it's all right," my mom said. "We like being lesbians."

My name is Zack, and I'm 11 years old. I live with my mom and Margie in New Jersey. My mom's name is Aimee. I also have a gray and white cat named Nicki. My mom bought her for me one Christmas.

When I'm not in school, I'm pretty busy doing things
with Margie and my mom. We practice for Little League
and go on picnics when the weather is warm. In the winter,
we go on sleigh rides. My mom is pretty cool, even though
she gives me a hard time if I don't wear a helmet when I'm
in-line skating.

I know that some kids think that having a lesbian mother is strange, or very different from the way they're being raised. But I think we live the same way any family does.

A person who has a sexual relationship with someone of the same sex is called gay, or homosexual. Women who are gay are also called lesbians. People who have relationships with someone of the opposite sex are called heterosexual, or straight.

I've heard some kids say really mean things about gay and lesbian people. They call them "fags" and "dykes." When I told my mother about this, she said, "The problem is not with us. It's with them. We're in a family where everybody loves each other, and that's what matters." That made me feel a lot better.

There are lots of different kinds of families. I'd be fine with a mom and a dad. I'd be fine with two dads. And I'm fine with two mothers. That's just the way it is.

MY MOM'S JOB is to help
people. I guess you could say
she's a teacher for adults. The
women in her class are on
welfare—the government gives
them money to help them pay
the bills. But these women
want to learn new skills and
get good jobs. My mom
teaches them how to work
with small children, so they
can get jobs in day care centers
or preschools.

My mom told me she met my dad when they were both in high school. They went out for seven years, then they got married. When I was five years old, they got divorced.

It didn't really matter to me, as long as I could be friends with both my mom and my dad. I still see my dad a lot. He lives nearby, so I can just walk to his house. He takes me to Shea Stadium, where we watch the New York Mets baseball team. And we go to the beach.

Around the time my parents got divorced, my mom met Margie. They had a lot in common. Margie also knows a lot about children. She works for toy companies. When these companies want to make a new toy, they ask for Margie's advice. She tells them how kids play with toys, and she shows them how to make the toys safe.

Margie already knew she was a lesbian when she met my mom. After my mother began spending time with Margie, she realized that she was a lesbian, too. My mom loved Margie and wanted to spend her life with her.

I guess I was lucky, because I liked Margie, too. She didn't live with us at first. She had her own apartment, three blocks away. But she ate just about every meal with us. After about a year, she moved in with me and my mom. The more I got to know her, the more I loved her. That's why I started calling her my second mother.

Margie's parents are like my grandparents. Her nieces and nephews are like my cousins. Margie's family gets together with my grandparents and cousins from my mom's family when I have a birthday party.

AT HOME, I DO SOME THINGS with my mom, and other things with Margie. My mom and I cook together. Not too long ago, she helped me make a quilt.

Margie and I like to play catch. Last year, Margie was my assistant baseball coach. I think she knew even more than the head coach. She loves sports. We watch baseball, hockey, soccer, and football on television together. Whenever the referee makes a bad call, she yells at the TV.

Sometimes my friends come over. Emily is my oldest friend—we like to play Monopoly together.

I also like to do things by myself. I draw a lot of pictures of houses. I like designing things. I wouldn't mind being an architect one day. I have jobs to do, too. We have an agreement at home. Since the cat was my present, she is my responsibility. I feed her and change her litter.

Every summer, my mom and Margie take me to Provincetown. It's this nice place on Cape Cod in Massachusetts. We do a lot of fun things there, like riding a bicycle built for two. I take turns riding first with Margie, then with my mom. We like to go to the beach, too. The last time we visited Provincetown, we also went whale watching.

On one of our vacations to Massachusetts, we went to the Boston Children's Museum. They had a special exhibit about different types of families. We saw an interesting poem by Aylette Jenness:

We may be related by birth or adoption or invitation.
We may belong to the same race or we may be of different races.
We may look like each other or different from each other.
The important thing is we belong to each other.
We care for each other.
We agree, disagree, love, fight, work together.
We belong to each other.

Afterwards, we had a talk about what the words meant. My mom and dad may not live together the way parents do in some families. But my mom and Margie and I are a family. My mom says families are people who feel they belong together. Well, I belong with my mom and Margie. And they belong with me.

Once in a while we go to events sponsored by Lambda Families of New Jersey. That's a group for gay parents and their children. This past Fourth of July, we went to Lambda Families' Independence Day picnic. The picnic was held on the lawn outside an Episcopal church in West Orange, New Jersey. But you didn't have to be a member of the church to attend the picnic. People came from all over the state, to see old friends and have fun.

The parents were all sitting around talking about their children—what schools they go to, their doctors, that kind of stuff. Little boys and girls were running around all over the grass, splashing in a kiddie pool and eating hot dogs. I was the oldest kid there. I played games with the little kids. I felt like I was their camp counselor.

EVERY YEAR AT THE END OF JUNE, my family goes to the
Gay Pride Parade in New York City. Gay men and lesbians
from all over the country march together, along with their
friends and families, down Fifth Avenue, the busiest street in
the city. Everywhere you look there are hundreds of people—
marching in the parade and lined up on the sidewalks.
I skate the whole way. Of course, my mom makes me
wear a helmet. But underneath, I wear a rainbow-colored
bandanna. The rainbow colors are a symbol of gay pride.

I like having a big audience to watch me skate. And it's
great getting the exercise.

This year, though, I saw something I didn't like. Some people were yelling at the marchers. They were saying that gay people are sick. Others were screaming that gays deserve to die from AIDS. A few guys were waving a Nazi flag. That's really terrible! During World War II, the Nazi government in Germany killed Jewish people, gay people, and other people the Nazis thought were different.

Some people who don't like gay people say that if your mother or father is gay, you'll become gay, too. That makes me laugh. My mother's gay, but I'm not my mother. I'm me. I plan to get married to a woman and have my own family one day. And I know my mom and Margie will be proud grandmothers.

I think people who say they hate gays don't even know what a gay person is like. Have they ever talked to a gay person? If they did, they wouldn't hate gay people anymore.

My mom told me, "If you're not ashamed and you don't hide, there's nothing to be ashamed about."

Still, I feel funny when I hear people saying bad stuff about gays. At the school I used to go to, a lot of kids said the word "fag" all the time. I didn't say anything to them. I was afraid that if they found out my mother was gay, things would be harder for me. They wouldn't exactly beat me up. But they'd make my time at school miserable.

One day, one of my friends used the word "faggot." I knew that he was a nice kid. I thought that maybe he used this word because nobody had told him it is mean. So I spoke up.

"Don't say 'faggot,'" I told him. "My mother's gay, and that really offends me."

As soon as I said something, I knew I did the right thing. Like I said, he was a nice kid. And he didn't want to lose me as a friend.

"I'm really sorry," he said. "I didn't know. Really, I didn't mean to offend you."

I went home happy that day. I felt a sense of relief, like I got a weight off my shoulders. And you know what? He's still my friend today.

WHEN I MEET OTHER KIDS from divorced families, I feel lucky. My dad and my mom are still friendly. He's really cool, and never says ignorant things about gay people. Even though I live with my mom and Margie, I get to see my dad a lot.

My dad's name is Lee, and he's a chef. He lives with his second wife, Laura. She's a pharmacist. They have a 10-month-old baby named Ariel. I try to visit my little sister at least twice a week. I like her a lot. She's really energetic. She tries to talk to me in her own language. Every time I come into the room, she holds out her arms, wiggles her fingers, and smiles.

My mom and Margie have some good news. They're going
to have a baby, too.

I'll be almost 12 years older than my new brother or sister.
But my mom and Margie told me there's nothing to worry
about. My mom is 11 years older than one of her sisters.
And Margie has a sister who is 12 years younger than she is.

Now, you might be wondering how a lesbian couple has a baby. There are a number of ways. First my mom and Margie read a lot of books. Then they talked to their doctors. The doctors arranged for Margie to have a medical procedure, sort of like an operation, but not as complicated. When it was over, Margie was pregnant.

I asked my mom why Margie was having the baby instead of my mom having it. She told me Margie had always wanted to experience giving birth to a child. Since my mom had already given birth to me, it was Margie's turn.

Even though Margie and I sometimes disagree, she says she's enjoyed raising me. Now she and my mom will raise a new child together.

I know that having a baby in the house will be tough sometimes. I'm not looking forward to waking up at two o'clock in the morning when the baby's crying. I am looking forward to playing with the baby. Since I already have a little sister, I'd love to have a little brother.

Whether the baby is a boy or girl, though, I'm going to be the big brother. When he or she needs advice, I'll have an answer. I'm sure that one day my brother or sister will hear someone say something cruel about how we have lesbian mothers. I'll say all the things my mom and Margie have said to me.

If there's one lesson I'd want a kid to know, it's that gay people are pretty much the same as anybody else. I feel lucky to have the home I have and the people there who care about me.

AFTERWORD

Several months after Zack was interviewed for this book, he once again became a brother to a little girl.

Dewey Margaret was born to Aimee and Margie on New Year's Day, 1996. Zack was delighted with this addition to his family. He offered to help with the baby any way he could. He helps dress his little sister, and he's also learning how to change diapers.

Although he's often busy with schoolwork, sports, friends, and other activities, he tries to spend time with Dewey. Sometimes, while Aimee and Margie relax in the living room, Zack takes the baby into his room. He likes to play rock songs on the radio for her.

Since Dewey was born, everyone in the family feels closer than ever. And, with a baby to play with, they're having fun!

Information about
GAY AND LESBIAN PARENTS

Gay men and lesbians fall in love with and have relationships with people of their own sex. Two men or two women may choose to live together as a family, sometimes raising children.

There are many ways gay people become parents. Aimee had her son Zack when she was married, before she lived with Margie. Often, gay couples or single gay men or lesbians choose to adopt a child. Aimee and Margie had a child together through a medical procedure called *artificial insemination*. This is a way that a woman becomes pregnant without any sexual contact.

In the past, gay parents often feared discrimination—unfair treatment because they were gay. They did not "come out," or tell people they were gay. Some lesbian mothers have had to fight for the right to keep custody of their children.

Many people in American society still fear or hate gay people. Each gay family deals with the situation differently. When Zack started school, Aimee and Margie introduced themselves to teachers, administrators, and other parents. They gave others a chance to get to know them.

Children who are raised by lesbian or gay parents are not different from children whose parents are not gay. Margie and Aimee believe that the most important thing for children is to have parents who love them and take care of them.

GLOSSARY

custody (CUSS-toe-dee)—the legal right of a parent to have his or her children live with that parent

discrimination (dis-crih-mih-NAY-shun)—unfair treatment based on something such as sexual identity, race, or disability

dyke (dike)—a lesbian; the term is often considered mean or offensive

fag—a gay man; the term is often considered mean or offensive

gay—a word used to describe men and women who are attracted to people of the same sex. *See* homosexual

heterosexual (HET-er-oh-sex-you-uhl)—attracted to someone of the opposite sex. *See also* straight

homosexual—attracted to someone of the same sex. *Homosexual* and *gay* are words that mean the same thing.

lesbian (LEZ-be-un)—a woman whose feelings of love and attraction are for women

straight—an informal term for heterosexual

For Further READING

Holbrook, Sabra. *Fighting Back: The Struggle for Gay Rights.* New York: E.P. Dutton, 1987.

Jenness, Aylette. *Families: A Celebration of Diversity, Commitment, and Love.* Boston: Houghton Mifflin, 1990.

Newman, Lesléa. *Heather Has Two Mommies.* Boston: Alyson Publications, 1991.

Pellegrini, Nina. *Families Are Different.* New York: Holiday House, 1991.

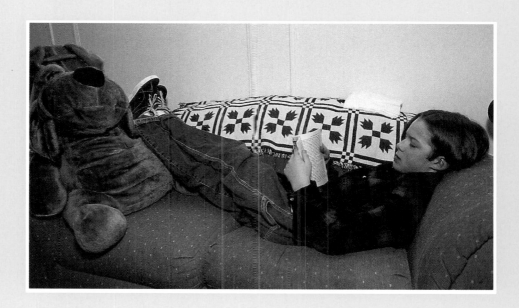

RESOURCES

Center Kids
208 W. 13th Street
New York, NY 10011
(212) 620-7310

Gay and Lesbian Parents Coalition International
P.O. Box 50360
Washington, DC 20091
(202) 583-8029

Lamda Legal Defense and Education Fund
666 Broadway, 12th Floor
New York, NY 10012
(212) 995-8585

Lavender Families Resource Network
P.O. Box 21567
Seattle, WA 98111
(206) 325-2643

National Gay and Lesbian Task Force
2320 17th Street NW
Washington, DC 20009-2702
(202) 332-6483